The speaker of these poems, sometimes with urgent pressured speech, sometimes with a cool remove, wants to tell us something. And we want to listen because what they say is like what we were just thinking. Or maybe like what we once thought. Once felt. Once did. Like that and yet different. This person's way of being is inimitable. As is ours. Yet their words insist themselves into being something we were about to say. The words came out of their mouth and entered our language-primed minds by way of the eyes which read: "Each day / I negotiate another way to live." The associative leaps (circumstantially tangential) between being and becoming keep taking us to that place where: "The word queer / is barbwire strung across pink sky and snow, / larkspur and lupine rising from pelvis." Sometimes poems teach us how to be. Sometimes they simply let us be who we were all along. These poems brilliantly do both. I'm dazzled by the depths they reach. By the brightness of the language. The sharpness of the blade they use to carve a new world from the old.
—Mary Jo Bang, Judge's citation for Omnidawn's 2022 1st/2nd Poetry Book Contest

Modernity has degraded the ancient complexities of the erotic more deeply understood, not eros as servile to sexuality, but eros as the body's ingathering of the world's myriad vitalities—the same world which gathers our vital selves into it. In Kelly Weber's *You Bury the Birds in My Pelvis* the privative prefix a- spreads wild is loosestrife wisdoms: asexual, aromantic. In the queerplatonic lyric consciousness of these poems praise becomes primary imperative. Praise of the other, praise of the all, praise of "every kind of sinful love /that's love even without bodies conjoining." The hope isn't to hack the body's troubling facts, nor is it to resolve its mysteries into dogma; the hope is "to find the words for your queerness," for all of our queernesses, so that we can hear, as this poet hears, the finchsong found singing in the marrow. Here disease works its dithyramb through the nerves, but the admission of pain allows sorrows seldom shared to garland themselves into a form of ~~~~ all, if we dare, can

wear. "I've risked sharing my breath with you." Yes, it's true: these poems inspire.
—Dan Beachy-Quick, author of *Variations on Dawn and Dusk*

"Morning pinks/the plains ice. /You bury the birds in my pelvis/and say my name." And so begins Kelly Weber's stunning *You Bury the Birds in My Pelvis*, which approaches memory through difficult burials where maternal landscapes are "acidic ash in the world" and "wood smoke," all in search of "little bones" that "heal fastest after a break." The speaker, indeed, never stops searching for flight and escape from coyotes and "windbreak woods burned" by redefining their own "Queerplatonic" which is sometimes "Snakeskin curled like celluloid/under the tongue" and "cactus lungs splintered truck nested with swallows." A daring collection that celebrates what unraveling can reveal about the will of self-invention, Weber is a determined and resilient present even when looking back at the harshest terrains, for "I am making a page."
—Rosebud Ben-Oni, Alice James Award Winner of *If This Is the Age We End Discovery*

Kelly Weber's extraordinary work is a remarkable testament to the power of language and of vulnerability. Lush and sensual, *You Bury the Birds in My Pelvis* is an essential addition to aspec literature. Weber presents asexuality and queerness as a continual journey of exploration both of the self and of the self's relationships to the body and to the wider community. It is particularly illuminating that this is a journey with "no easy articulation;" rather, it is "always a poem in the gap between leap and arrival, exhale." In these luminous poems, Weber leads the reader to seek "permission for a more honest language" to know themselves, celebrating the beauty of those who know themselves best in "a language made of everything that doesn't fit."
—Emma Bolden, author of *The Tiger and the Cage: A Memoir of a Body in Crisis*

PREVIOUSLY PUBLISHED

We Are Changed to Deer at the Broken Place (Tupelo Press, 2022)

You Bury the Birds in My Pelvis

Cover art by Emily Goodhart

Cover design by Laura Joakimson
Interior design by Laura Joakimson
Cover typeface: Marion
Interior typeface: Marion and Hightower

Library of Congress Cataloging-in-Publication Data

Names: Weber, Kelly (Poet), author.
Title: You bury the birds in my pelvis / Kelly Michelle Weber.
Description: Oakland, California : Omnidawn Publishing, 2023. | Summary:
   "Set against a rural plains landscape of gas stations, wind, and
   roadkill bones on highways, You Bury the Birds in My Pelvis is a love
   letter to the nonbinary body as a site of both queerplatonic intimacy
   and chronic illness. Through art and friendship, the poems imagine
   alternatives to x-rays, pathologizing medical settings, and other forms
   of harm. At the place where radiological light and meadow meet--at the
   site where the asexual speaker's body meets feather and fox
   skeleton--what love poem becomes possible? When the body is caught in
   both medical crisis and ecological catastrophe, how is a poetry
   fashioned despite--and out of--endings? How can a self-portrait be a
   form of agency when so many harmful images of the sick queer body are
   made by others? You Bury the Birds in My Pelvis explores these questions
   with forms that reach across the page, the plainspoken prose poem
   becoming its own strange field. In a mix of short poems and longer lyric
   sections that navigate insurance systems and complicated rural
   relationships to queerness, the speaker does not find easy answers.
   Rather, they find ways to make a life: with foreheads pressed together,
   with antlers in the grass"-- Provided by publisher.

Identifiers: LCCN 2023019299 | ISBN 9781632431240 (trade paperback)
Subjects: LCGFT: Poetry.
Classification: LCC PS3623.E39456 Y68 2023 | DDC 811/.6--dc23/eng/20230501
LC record available at https://lccn.loc.gov/20230192

Published by Omnidawn Publishing, Oakland, California
www.omnidawn.com
10 9 8 7 6 5 4 3 2 1
ISBN: 978-1-63243-124-0

You Bury the Birds in My Pelvis

Kelly Weber

OMNIDAWN PUBLISHING
OAKLAND, CALIFORNIA
2023

for you, always, and the rain in our teeth

CONTENTS

INSTEAD OF ANOTHER X-RAY

let your hands pull my ribs back today.
Not light dividing bone from the softer shadows
but your voice slitting me
from pelvis to chin, hiding among the hollows
feather after feather
like the yellow flower my mother painted
floating above the blue hills
while I slept under morphine, winter cloud.
Once I cared for an ashbed full of animal skeletons,
my throat swallowing fistful after fistful of glass.
All the fossils soft enough
to still be marrow instead of rock.
When I cradle the skull of the mare
again, you kneel beside me, both of us holding
the twelve-million-year-old body
giving birth to a stillborn foal cupped in her hips.
One hoof pressed against the absence
her heart makes. Morning pinks
the plains ice. You bury the birds in my pelvis
and say my name.
Our bones remember water. Each day
I negotiate another way to live.

/

HOW TO DRAW YOURSELF AS DAUGHTER

Begin with you and your mother following the bleeding fox
across the field. No, begin with your mother weeping—
birth this story with your body in the mirror, herringboned
and hemorrhaging into girl. Your mother's hand
cupped over yours, arcing your arm across red fur.
Voice a new moon
falling into black water. Study in graphite
how girls dress their marrow in blood here,
fasten white buttons across red flannel
and bury dawn behind the sternum. Let's say
in this little frame of paper
you step toward her
and anything could happen
before sunrise, antlers in your throat. Frost and rust
revealing every father's tractor on the night highway
a mouth of needles. Grip the pencil
and look into your friend's eyes
as you both count down to state
the animals you are. The word queer
is barbwire strung across pink sky and snow,
larkspur and lupine rising from pelvis.
Return here to your mother, the fox
dragging itself across frozen grass, the widened eye, the small
red spooling beneath your hands
that don't know what to call forgiveness,
what to call mercy. Beneath the fur, beneath the ice
you must know how to draw the skeleton first.

WHEN I WATCHED MY MOTHER PAINT

her mother as a woman in a high-backed chair / with a northern flicker beak piercing my grandmother's side / I stayed small on the floor behind her / knees tucked beneath chin / a daughter watching her / invent lungs from sky long dark hair falling past / the painted woman's breasts / wrapped in thorns / buds strung across her throat / blue and green -singed squirrel-tail brushes harvested from roadkill / I am watching how a woman learns to forget / even her children to fall into / herself enough to make a second body / how a barbed tongue hunts whatever sweetness lives / between breaths / what my mother would not say of her mother / was a tongue I could not find my way through / a hummingbird trying to drink / from the red plastic flowers on the chest / of my childhood / bathing suit / blessing the air with thirst / and sugar I could not offer / she used to hunt in the woods with her father / every throat bowing / inside her / crosshairs the bullet that broke the morning to pieces / each red testament laying itself across the snow / during the war her father shot a snake between the legs of a man / who said he wanted to die / just to watch the blood splatter his shocked alive face / the first time I ripped the skin off my thumb / I was relieved / as if I'd torn the moon's face / and found just a watt bulb behind it / bruising phosphorous in my eyes / with my fists / on the basement floor / beneath my mother and her mother / arguing desperate circles in the kitchen / I watch her draw the brush down the canvas / there are times I am still in the bedroom doorway / looking at red smears on my mother's sheets / my voice saying *mom, mom, mom* like a pulse / clothespinned to a bird's wing / so this is the portrait of a woman's closed mouth / I return to / this is how I watch my mother's back / bent toward the canvas / in this basement studio / with its cold cement floor / and ground-level window / this is how/ how I pluck a single blonde strand / of sunlight tangled on a branch / on the other side of glass / wrap it around my finger / remember that some of the most acidic ash in the world is wood smoke / that when a forest burns / the ghost of all that green / paint that proves beauty is always this close / to poison

PORTRAIT OF CRIB WITH COYOTE SKULL INSIDE

1.

Because again the bar with steer horns
mounted above the bottles and mirror, ranchers with barb-
scarred knuckles clutching glasses
of whiskey, their dark lapels
gathered like ravens at their throats.
Because snow gathering in my mouth
from the street, forsythia caught behind my teeth.
Because my legs in tights, because fox and rabbit
sewn with sawdust and posed in pursuit around the room,
because my friend photographing flowers in her hair
and titling it theft—petal, long strand—
because the smell of aftershave and cigarette leaning forward,
someone pressing their breath to the back of my neck,
someone's brother or someone's father or someone's son,
a door made of wrists I have chewed my way through—

2.

Because again the eyes of my mother
in the doe I approach in the woods.
My arm around her neck
pressing her long face soft as rust
against my cheek. Because once I used her hand mirror
to peer between my legs, pearls
studding the folds of pink lace
around the glass.
Like the flies that scripture her tongue
when I find her, hooves dangling off the flatbed.
Because my hands trying to lift the body
heavy as a child. Because for any hoofed thing
life must be a balance of panic and poise,
stillness before buckle into snow. Because it is my hand
on the knife, sawing hide from muscle and undoing
mother, your spine.

BLOOD FIRSTS

I bury my bloody underwear in the trash out back where coyotes yip at night. When we talk about the girl who drowned in the reservoir on the edge of town, I pick my skin open like a dare: first a little flap, then a sudden rush of red. I tell my father my friend said a construction worker on the roof of the school shouted *nice ass* at her, he says she wishes she got that kind of attention. A boy bites my lip for seven minutes and I feel every failure to want. I bleed for almost two months straight, like I could leak enough into a girl. My father loads a gun, aims at the crows that circle and dive at him to guard their nests. My grandmother talks about wanting to keep daughters small, little baby heads cradled in her palms, each breath needing her to go on living. I dream wet hair tangled in beer cans. I dream a girl with headlights for eyes, a throat churning cigarettes, broken glass under blue. I walk down the hall to the steer skull my mother drew, pull it down. I peer through the paper sockets to see my young mother narrow as a birch, leaning over her art with such fierce attention. The first time I put my feet in the stirrups and let the blue gown fall open to nipple and navel, I stain the paper sheet a little. The first time I try the word *asexual* in my mouth and the man smirks out back behind the bar, his eyes taking me as a challenge. I stumble over railroad tracks to the reservoir, draw nude after nude I don't know how to need, draw the cross and the doll left for the girl where the deer sometimes come to drink streaked with headlights. My mother and I care for the road-broken things in our garage for long as we can. Little bones heal fastest after a break.

PORTRAIT AS MID-2000S GIRL WITHOUT A BOYFRIEND

When you cry the whole summer because she no longer wants
to speak to you, I realize there are loves we aren't allowed a name for
yet. Words for us like the way the teeth won't quite close
when we try to zip up each other's backs in the regular-size section
of the dress store with antelope heads mounted on the wall
above the wooden sign about God's love and sins of the flesh.
When you miss her so much I can hear you trying to catch your breath,
your face pressed into her old torn sweater, I hold still and quiet
to let you draw me the way you used to draw her. Enough
to catch every *girl* four boys croon on a bad MP3 rip
through the apartment wall. The nest of baby rabbits you brought in
to sleep next to your chest—lifted shaking from the matted grass—
watching us with wet dark eyes from their little cage.
I imagine undressing my wrists for you, undoing each bead of the friendship
bracelet to offer my blue-pulsed veins for you to press fingertips to—
not like a kiss, not like the girl who arranged broken glass
into the word *love* in art class and washed grout from her hands
to reveal them covered in line after line of blood, but like a river
big enough to hold you in its cold silver noise, an ultrasound
echoing everything we don't tell our mothers. You draw me
out like this—smiling even when I'm always a breath away from sorry,
hair cropped short, breasts hidden, not dancing with boys
at the party, hugging a wall with you. Each of us
trying to name the way a friend hauls herself out of the pool
sluicing water across the edge, ankle rhinestoned with chlorine,
and slaps away barefoot without saying our name
ever again—what do we call that kind of loss? I know
what it is to harm myself, to have no word for heal. Last year
two girls stole each other's hands at prom
behind everyone's backs. It is not bodies I want, but how they let
one another close enough to touch—to thieve
some safety in each other. You measure the distance
from my eye to my cheek, philtrum to lip, the way I count
your freckles not as something to desire

but as something so wholly yourself. Not as something to ache for
but to be so fully known. You draw the silo in moonlight
behind our teeth, September silenced of cicadas and sermons,
palms pressed above each other's breasts
asking nothing of each other but to keep our secrets.
You draw us breathing like my aunt
setting her birth house on fire and watching it fall to ash,
the field quickening into a line of flame, every rabbit fleeing
in a streak of tremble and muscle before smoke so thick
it formed a throat heavy with heartbeat, a language.

SNAKE-JAWED EPITHALAMIUM

Again I watch a cousin   fitted for a wedding gown
      lace and strings tightened   across the back, whale elegy
written across the spine   Fingers clasped around a bouquet
      Again the questions everyone   poses to me
when will it be my turn?   Confess—
      who's the special   *someone in my life?*   Someday
I will find the right person   At the barn reception
      bride and groom dance   wind stirring blue ribbons
in the rafters, the antler chandelier   mounted deer head
      I pitch bottles   against a fence
in the field out back   lobbing glass
      shattering into the grass   Cigarettes flaring in the dark
couples running off into the windbreak trees   I walk barefoot
      to the edge of the lake   find a condom
-thin snakeskin   raise it to moonlight
      wonder if I am human if I am broken   frigid queer girl
the dead deer rises again   breathing in the dark blue
      I step into water   peel the moon from my body
practicing love   with every mirror I can shed

QUEERPLATONIC (WINDBREAK CROWN)

Queerplatonic: imprecise definition for tongue and jaw, two latched things.
Like, queerplatonic we hit the doe anyway, skidding on black ice. Her
blood on your headlights, your hand cradling her jaw when you tell me
you love me as a friend. My palm on her scapula, both our arms holding
her for a moment before we drag her onto the shoulder of January snow.
Queerplatonic our breath puffing clouds into a sky nailed shut with
stars. Queerplatonic how we tell no one. How a body twists open this
way, hungering & stunned with light.

/

You and I grew up in the same hungered fist
of the plains: crosses
and cow skulls nailed to barn walls,
anti-abortion billboards nailed above bullet-ridden stop signs
on the edge of town,
frost starring the sign of the shop run by two men
no one called a couple.
Where a girl is the space she leaves:
severed umbilicus, trail of gunpowder
through the brain of a mare. Where a girl
is no-trespassing signs nailed with antlers,
dogs chasing trucks down gravel roads
stars cinching frost to breast, sternum. The word *queer*
a boot snugged over a weather-eaten gray fence post
with a dried snake dangling from the barb
-wire: pinned by a loggerhead shrike
or somebody's son.

/

Queerplatonic: gold feed pouring into silo on a sunless winter day.
Meadowlark whistling a hole in the pink morning
to escape a coyote.

/

To escape the coyote smiles
        of people in school, pretend to like a boy.
Act like *hot* means something besides your neck flushed
        when he asks you to dance and you say yes
then neither of you move from the bleachers
        because you don't think you can sway
into that much of a lie.

To escape being branded by a word
bury it in the frozen dirt
beneath bluestem, until you hit ash
from millions of years ago,
until you hit mammoth tooth

until you hit your tongue
and then cover it with howl, bird wing, little song.

/

when I was old enough to know the song
              of how I should want to kiss someone—anyone—
my father and I drove out to see meteors
              streak their silent blue deaths in the field.
Your father brought you the jawbone of a fox
              he found in a field. We pass it back
and forth touching the loose music
              of the teeth, talking for hours
where light divides the midnight between us.

/

Queerplatonic: you and I learning about each other in cars
during long rides to football games. Ice storm closing the distance.

Queerplatonic: our grandfather's hands inside the houses they build
leveling beam after beam. Then a match set to the wood.

/

The year the windbreak woods burn. The first time you smile at me across the circle of bodies in teen bible study. Long drives with hawks standing still in the wind above the highway, sky staved with powerlines. The motel bed we share overnight in Iowa without even letting our spines touch. Your keys dangling in the ignition. Your bra tossed across the bed while you shower. The geese crying in the dark above our heads. Our whistles to each other behind the trees when we play wolves with our friends at night. The abandoned barns and houses we creep into, rafters falling, minuses of sunlight strewn on the floor—mouse bones on the hardwood. Wallpaper dangling in strips of black mold where a wife once kneaded dough in the kitchen, where we trace circles with our breath and our index fingers in the frost gathered on the glasstop. The table where a father once skinned deer, opening their bellies on the wood. The books we read to each other in the dark. How I do not want your body but only want to go on listening to you talk about paragraphs, stanzas, how you crack back each like a rib cage to touch the raw heart inside. Your journals poemed into dragonfly wings, whole books better than I'll ever write, line after line after line. How you never make me feel emptied. How I have set each thing slowly into your palms for safekeeping, like my mind could always have a safe place to land.

/

Inside the arches of canyon and land
        we are still finding the language of love
as blood tether, as close reading of a poem
            to find the words for what we are.
        If it takes me years to learn the words *asexual*,
aromantic, how am I ever supposed
            to join tongue and hinge into a way
to be whole, to know how to describe
        your small chest pressed to mine
at the high school dance, I in a suit
            in a photograph of us I'll find years later
and tear in half, afraid of every happiness in my face?

/

Halfway to the barn dance behind our high school
       where you and I found each other

your hips beside mine
       we each look out the windows pearled with our breath

and I am suddenly afraid
       of everything I might want, aware of your warm

side, aware that my unwanting body
       may just make an exception for you, afraid of the word

hammering louder and louder in my head.
       And when we dance, your hands guiding mine

you swing me so hard I think my scapula will come loose
       in the smell of old hay and horse sweat,

where people testify to their absolution from queer thoughts
       to a chorus of *amen* and upturned palms

and I study the small knobs of your vertebrae
       beneath your sweat-soaked gray shirt, wanting

to praise your whole skeleton right there in front of everyone
       like setting fire to a swirl of gold seed in a silo

just to watch the flames burn
       right through the moon like celluloid.

/

Queerplatonic: Snakeskin curled like celluloid
    under the tongue. The tongue and all that language is.

/

that is, I try not to sing a ghost echo between every line
          every line another part of a rib cage knit together
when he asks you to dance like you're his
          his coyote cry
I want to show him how *girl* can be soft as baby clothes
          clothed in this tongue
wrapped around knives—tell me how I find you
          a knife made of light: your name
like a prayer, how in that small town of men
          my winter my wind my prayer
calling us good wives, good mothers close around us
          close your heart around my hands
I want to hide in the hands of my disobedient friends
          obedient to every sky
like you, I want to go down to the river naked
          naked as a river I don't want to like you
reciting Jesus's words backward
          the devil's back a lullaby to hold me
I want this to be you
          I want to be my own definition of want
I watch girls vanish themselves in marriages to men
          dawn a marriage of birds to landscape in vanish
and you and I, watching rabbits dart under the tractor
          trying not to beg like rabbits' heartbeats for their life
saying each other's names like sisters, like claimed
          the years it has taken to claim my queer life
that I never tell you the truth—
          tell the edges of our bodies mawed
with our hips so close together
          close as gone
and alive held in the palms I
          I palm all our aliveness like a dragonfly humming
keep fighting to share one more breath one more dance
          once more once more once more

/

when we dance the small cries   of the fiddle
are a name for water   I cannot stop pulling
through my heart   its blood   each match   struck under the
tongue

/

Struck tongue—I have never known how to read the sonnet
maybe because I've never known how to read a face
as beautiful. But I've learned
your sweet face, your purple hair, eye sockets bruised sleepless,
how to read how you carry grief, how you send me
all the poems you write, the poem you are,
because we can't help but read closely what we come to love.
Like the day before we say goodbye
when we drive around pointing at shredded blue-silver cans
twisted in the horse fences. Your hands on my wrist
clasping a watch against my pulse, a dial
opening blood like the barn doors we hid behind.
The cold in my lungs.

/

queerplatonic: cactus lungs splintered truck nested with swallows

/

Praise the swallows nesting in the barn church where I hide my tongue

Praise our small breaths next to each other as she testifies
        to her conversion therapy making her into a proper wife

Praise semis and tractors roaring down the road before dawn

Praise the fox slipping away from a father's gun down by the fence

Praise gas station coffee and florescent lights in the dark
        beyond the truck stop windows

Praise every kind of sinful love
        that's love even without bodies conjoining

Praise trachea cloudbank, steel rose shiver

Praise the lavender tea you brew while you wear your red flannel
sweater,
buttons glistening like bone next to me
on the old midwestern couch

Praise horses galloping in the fields at night
        the sound of hooves echoing over highway and dry creekbed

Praise friendship and sunlight glittered in smashed blue bottles

Praise the small candles we light for someone's stillborn

Praise every time I almost confess my praise to you,
        swallowing words like bruises ringed in taillight,
        broken exhaust pipe driving a hole in horizon

/

How, when you drive away for the last time
and we can't find the language for the end,
we can't find the language for how we loved
each other, I want to open my mouth to say
I'm a tongue of larkspur, I'm a prairie aster
helixing open, I'm a socket
meeting its bone, I'm cloud opening on the back of a dragonfly I—

/

queerplatonic a dragonfly spotted with blue paint
queerplatonic two boards nailed together
queerplatonic a goodbye breathing into a hush of birds

/

Like trees hushed into small bodies of birds in winter
I have learned to language this as *enough*

that the person I so often write to
is the person I once was

when we didn't say we loved each other
before we stopped saying anything to each other at all,

hooves in the dark, another soft breathing at the window.

/

Instead of hooves in the dark and the bright V of blood on the highway

Instead of your family disowning you

Instead of the shotgun echoing across the empty fields at night

Instead of your brother saying *the sin of a homosexual lifestyle*

Instead of making our bed with you

Instead of my horizon breaking its back across your mouth

Instead of our hips and thighs hugged close as period and comma
on couch

Instead of winter sewing heartbeats onto our tongues

Instead of a wooden cross fished from the backs of our molars

Instead of our collarbones across the night sky

Instead of hiding small prairie rattlers in your soft breathing your throat

Instead of your running every morning outside the house through fog

Instead of my skin hunger yawning like craters of slag and river
    I have flown over, virga streaked above mountains

Instead of our bodies slow dancing at a reception in the armory

Instead of dawn leaking from the vein of my arm

Instead of a drowned mare I hauled from the reservoir

Instead of this canyon between us blood tender as an embrace

Instead of the deer you let into the room, antlers at the window

                              I say nothing

                         /

I say nothing

and I keep living in the prairie where deer kneel in the
fields. Needles of windbreak pines shivering with late winter rain. A
systole of wings. A barn with a blood smear on the wall the next field
over. Rumor of pumas at night. I wake to the sound of wheels and wind
on the highway, rattling coils of rusted wire shivering in truck-beds, the
hissing gap in the window above the flannel sheets. A cow full of milk
begins to cry. I name the magpies, birches glistening with ice all around
us, the animals edited down to bone. I start to say a word, take it back,
bury it again.

NOCTURNE WITH KEYS CLENCHED BETWEEN KNUCKLES

—sorry, what I'm trying to say is
when I tell you my vagina once prolapsed, I mean
it's amazing what doesn't hurt. My chest when he pushed
his weight off me in self-defense class,
after he grabbed my hair and pinned me
to the hardwood, sweaty gasoline-blonde arm
shoved against me until
I tasted iron. My breast
heavy in my hand as the rain-stunned ringneck dove
I cradled behind the house
before the hawk carried it over
still blue water.
Once my mother
watched a painter bite her own wrist to stain the canvas.
Bleeding a little after the speculum,
do I smear the air with succulent rust
walking home tonight?
If a man keeps pace with me across the street
does he do it on purpose or does he not notice
how I hide my panic
like a blank cartridge in the skull of a deer?

ODE TO HIS KNIFE COLLECTION

Once he pressed a knife against my throat / just to prove his control
to our friends / his palm on the smooth bone / and maple burled handle
/ riveted with iron eyes / stopping just short of my carotid / his green
eyes / staring into mine / I kept the silence for years / of the boys who
asked me in front of everyone / if I liked to swallow hairy balls / if I
wanted to put them in my mouth / and the boy who always wanted to
explain steel to me / who showed me each knife / in his basement room
/ that used to be a mortuary / where the bodies used to lie / buried like
coals in the chest / asking when I told him / I had a nightmare / of
someone looking through my window at night / if it was him / who
told me his father / once beat up a man to win his mother / once saw
wolf tracks approaching his fence / and a man's tracks walking away /
when he talked about men who cratered faces for their wives / I think
he meant he wanted / to rescue me from my queerness / to feel like a
man / and when he asked me again and again / that summer all the
roads flooded / I learned every way to say no / is the wrong way / too
gentle to count / or too harsh not to wound / the angry boy crowned in
his father's cigarette smoke / If I cut open this skin / will a pelt thicken
the wound? / If our friends stop talking to me / because I refuse to talk
to him anymore / if everyone they feel so sorry for him / for losing a
friend / if nothing happened / though I looked over my shoulder for
weeks / while people told me I was overreacting / if the sweetest meat
is in the throat / if I go back and lift a blade beneath my sternum / will
I find an animal beneath / still dragging my ribs and heart cords with
it? / Can I sever the wolf from its hunger? / Fear carried for so long in
the gut / becomes a diamond / soaked in embalming fluid / driftwood
smooth as an elbow / born on the back of blue water / across the fields
and the roads / o little glitterbacks / I open the door to you / and you
flash into a pulse / at the end of the story / where nothing happens /
except knife after knife growing under my tongue

PORTRAIT OF THE CHEST AS FOGGED MIRROR AND BALLPOINT TATTOO

or how I say the word *promise* like a knife folding behind the sternum
—we walk out of this bathroom together only when your breath is steady.
how you called my name like I knew how to say anything
that would make it okay to leave the moldy pink covenants of *pussy*
slut cunt gouged into each stall door like I could make everything outside of here
safer than this brute lullaby of rust & urine-burned air, brine-ringing each toilet
for queer girls like us— how you hid here and asked for the girl
in the too-large dragon shirt hiding her breasts like two unruly gods
& the school counselor brought me here —don't chew your lip
because that's what I do because you're the one who knows how
to live in the body to find the names
& the beauty for what other girls already smell on us, corseted
in razors and acne calling us worthless bitch
or saying nothing when boys tell me in class what they'd like down my throat.

I'm the one who's always trembled
like the doe I met in the bare field
lifting her head and wedging herself
shaking November drizzle from her fur
silence unzipped from a pulse.
we have been so afraid
to fail at pulling the little tail
at how we fail to want
how do our bodies
mean *cornered*?
her father pulled me aside
closed the door and undid
tattooed across his calf
the knotty fist of man muscle

but now I'm the one approaching you
breathing like a morning bruise
between me and the other deer
like shedding a sudden silver silhouette.
there is a way to exist before apology.
even of tampons
of the bloomed wound unclotting inside us.
in the correct ways.
come to mean *closet*,
like how at our friend's 13th birthday party
into a bedroom
his pants leg to show me the dragon
to watch my face watching
like a baby sewn tight under the skin,

each coarse hair fevering
my breath stilled
you once screamed underwater
each sound an empty
snapped off the lights
by light under the door, a hammered halo
until my face uncoupled into
going, you ask. I promise
will keep their bloody discipline
& I give you a thumb-printed peach
cradling a moon in each fist

its little match from the nickeled scales.
in the smell of cigarettes and sweat
alone in the pool
bubble. I once came to this bathroom
and watched my face in the mirror
until my pupils swelled
fangs. how are we supposed to keep
only our hearts
under our ribs.
stolen from a blue bowl
we step into hooves and water.

EXPLICATION OF THE POET'S BREASTS

needled with blue damselflies[1]

                          veins in the mirror[2]

               -ed nipples the areola[3] red-brown as the foothills

                     backshadowed[4] with blue rain[5]

                     falsing[6] the peaks

heartbeat[7] under muscled fat

---

[1] I can't write about breasts without thinking of damselflies stinging the surface of water.

[2] When I came out to my mother as ace and aro, never wanting to marry or have children, she had already looked up the definitions. That summer the cicadas in the single aspen ended their humming all at once.

[3] Scan the rhythm of blood.

[4] Once I overheard my mother say she wasn't sure at times I was really a girl. I felt like a drowned witch, hurt and confirmed.

[5] I made myself forget. My first period: punctuation closing a sentence. Each time a cishet man misgendered me or described the way my body failed to perform as woman, I wanted to latch my jaws into his throat. Each time someone spent a whole conversation treating me as genderblurred I felt annoyed but also—pleased? By what? Truth? Accuracy? Possibility? I—

[6] Perhaps this is an exegesis of all the ways I keep trying to hack into my body. Like if I just keep trying, I'll have a way to articulate gender instead of an owl pellet taken apart in my palm.

[7] Tender, the mouth's bruise I circle again and again in the mirror.

thunder honeying[8] into estrogen[9] horizon

each swaying tit and gland[10]

a stretchmarked[11] chapel swelled with tongues

gravity's[12] gelatinous bells milkless

and godless[13] as fossils

pair of red eyes unveiled[14] blinkless

unsuckled teats

undone[15] at the ghost

---

[8] More than once I burst into sudden, inexplicable, uncontrollable sobs in front of dressing room mirrors when I sutured myself into something lacy, when my friends waited for me to step out fully girl. Sometimes I locked myself in for fifteen minutes, pretending I was trying on dress after dress while I actually hunched in my underwear waiting for the tears to stop, the AC to cool back down the tender pink of my eyes.

[9] I fantasize about cutting my breasts off. A sharp, painless blade severing me closer to what I really am.

[10] Every failure to arrive: as girl, as desiring others, as mouth, as tongue.

[11] Someone accidentally sent me a text meant for someone else, asking them to talk to me about how to be prettier, more feminine. Before the family party: You don't need to mention you're queer.

[12] The girls I loved with such the deepest hatred were the ones who ignored me. Or told me to close my eyes and trailed a knife blade over my palm without breaking the skin.

[13] They tried to teach me girl like they tried to teach me desire for. Like fitting language to a pair of scissors: say hot. Say want. Show your cleavage a bit. Baby teeth rewriting into screws.

[14] Sometimes, just for comfort, I lie back and cup each breast. Each one soft and heavy as a small sleepy hen, something both comforting to squeeze in the hand and to be touched this way. The nurse who examined my breasts one finger tap at a time, a massage with no desire but to make sure there was no cancer.

[15] Somedays I try to live with these breasts I mean poems. Other days I want to set them on fire.

heavy as an empty crib [16]

twinned[17] hives sagging into blood honey

nudging the sky's mouth open[18]

to beg[19] such a brutal thirst[20]

---

[16] Maybe that makes my chest an ars poetica.

[17] I turn this way and that in front of the mirror in a pair of black and white rattlesnake boots with my writer sister-friends watching, my breasts stretching my black shirt taut. I lift my chest a little higher, feel hiss and fang over ankle, every scale a vibrating comma.

[18] I wish I had a satisfactory label, after each one I tried out. For how I wanted to keep my pronouns and also kept spilling over the edges of the word girl. In fear I kept rewinding my terms. I thought, because I had arrived at no easy articulation, this was a failure to be queer enough, a failure to be body. Now perhaps I think there is always a poem in the gap between leap and arrival, exhale.

[19] My mother paints steer skulls on canvas over and over again. I try to say queer more easily in each conversation with her, fitting it to my tongue and body. Every attempt a compromise of precision in favor of honesty.

[20] No. Of blood.

ODE TO THE DRIFT GLASS NECKLACE
MY FRIEND GAVE ME

she said it's good / when you can finally find the words for your
queerness isn't it / and it was like finding finchsong braided in my
marrow / for the very first time / everyone needs someone / to do that
for them / give them permission for a more honest language / to live /
like every blue and green bottle sawing the lake shore / of my family's
blood / of every daughter who drank rat poison or liquor / could be
softened to wrists / accreting sun blades into mercy / every secret we
sank in the water / like forcing shut the teeth of a trap / -ped animal /
for years I have tried to fit / all the pieces of my gender / inside me /
almost all female / but still there has been / something else / speaking
out of me when I'm anemic / rusting into rumor of moon / fable-cored
girl who hated being called sir / then offered an apology wrapped in a
stare at my breasts / and a Jesus bookmark / hated being called ma'am
by strangers / avoided mirrors while naked / dressing as a skeleton or
gender ambiguous for Halloween / cutting my hair shorter and shorter
/ gender as girl with snake in her mouth / one breast cut off to let gush
from it / a fork-tongued doe / a language made out of everything that
doesn't fit / because I want to be as beautiful / as my friends think I am
/ when I can't get my hair cut for a long time / I hate the woman who
stares out of me / like a long-denied heir / of marrow and glass / but I
can make it through waiting / one more day / because my friends say /
my whole queer self is beautiful / because my best friend / makes me
feel soft enough / to live inside these long lacy sleeves / draw my knees
up to my chest / tender skin and black tights stretched taut / like I could
finally let someone / like her sleep against my side / like this / gently
breathing together / platonically / in our bodies / it has taken me this
long / to let the sharptoothed animal / of whatever gender I am / live
inside me like this / watching the stone on my chest / bounce in time
with my pulse / like my name / means both green / and any gender /
I'm born to / thigh teeming into rain / and pubic hair / ovaried meadow
/ the words I use for myself wide enough to hold / agave bloom and
panic / grass perennial / coneflower uncorseting my pronouns / into
greening tongues

JOKES ONLY ASEXUALS WILL UNDERSTAND {CLICK ON LINK TO OPEN NEW PAGE}

The punchline: cake.

My palm paused above the hot keyboard
realizing the word was real.

Once it rained a thousand dead birds
wings flopping on the ground like hands.

In the sex ed video two people grow up
into a set of mouths tonguing the air.

Any time people described [crush] [sex]
[romance] [attraction] [sexual frustration] to
me, I thought they were pretending or had
convinced themselves of the existence of
something fake. Then some of them married
the chapel lights bright. Each time they
described loving their partner making room in
the body for people I heard [ ] [ ] [ ] [ ] [ ] [ ] [ ] [ ]

The punchline: gods!

My mouth that doesn't kiss people: [   ]

When his hand brushed my breast
we pretended it was an accident after the lights came back.

Now you dip your chin in the mirror
and pluck for hours.

At D&D the man who wouldn't stop coming on to me
no matter how many times I said ace
leaned in the bathroom doorway to block me with a smile

when I tried to walk out. Said. *I want to make you feel uncomfortable.*

The punchline: dragons!

                My ass in sweat pants going for a run: [   ]

The first time I'm catcalled on the street
haunts every male voice afterwards
calling me from any proximal distance.

                    Steel scrape of the speculum hinging open.
                        He doesn't look at my face.

Oh you're so young you're in denial you don't even know what you
want!

                                The punch
                                line: [   ].

The asexual forum circulates warnings
not to click on certain links posted by incels.
Don't look at the photos.

                  If a sex-repulsed asexual girl with a libido
                          masturbates in a forest...
      Blur of blood against cochlea.

Link: rare catastrophe of feathers pouring from sky!

                When I lean back and stroke my clit
                I think about [   ].

Say there's a plate with a slice of cake on it.

                      Knees in bath water.

Sometimes the body just needs: intransitive verb.

I come back from a run and my friend calls me a little snack
in my sweat-soaked shirt. I think about chew,
swallow, tongue, eat while I leave the tap on.

guess what's up my sleeve / in the hand / in the hole!

synonyms for ace girl masturbating: one-handed grief practice.
fuse ending in tongue. coping mechanism as knife
sharpening on clouds.

navel and cellulite pooled with warm water
ventricles pounding pulse between thighs
sky full of wings threaded together by lightning

running running running running

LETTER TO AN INCEL FROM AN ACE GIRL

like my body is so easily confused with your anger. not the girl you follow down the street *like a newborn fawn* just to make her aware of you but the echoing steps behind, the ghost of want, desire shaped like silhouette. tonight I roll over and you're so close, I swear, I pluck your scapula, hang it in the window for a moon. another light by which to insist on my pulse, gravity.

/

writing out rejections to pickup lines / in sex ed
for homework / someone says don't you just love
to swallow / the whole bright ring / a mouth makes
what is a tongue / if not to taste
what is forbidden / but I only think
of the kind boy
stuffing paper in his mouth / he glances at me
and my raw fingers / and we keep
the secrets / by which wants like ours
are smuggled to adulthood / radared deep inside us
holding out my palm
for a sloppy wet coin / silver crusted from saliva
I'm told / to avoid masturbation / because it will make it harder
to love and please my husband / someday
horse rocking in the back of the throat / trojan
secret / eventually I want to want
but attraction never arrives / except as a sort of softening
into someone's kindness

/

chad chaser
degenerate female
repressed
self-deluded

biological clock
won't remain a virgin forever
won't remain a virgin for a 9 or 10 chad

      even you
don't believe me
              do you
      even you
          conflate action
and attraction
             even you
      name hymen
little god
      of rust and thumb

proof & proof & proof & proof & proof

     /

what are bodies for if not wanting to dissolve boundaries between them?
you follow someone to the end of this sentence, the hole where
punctuation   should go

and it's still just a way we unravel our veins, our nerve endings
      into tongues
licking our bodies back into the humming we are—
      finish this phrase: I look back over my shoulder at ____

if the word *you* is made only of vowels to open
the throat and then close it enough to keep something close
      then who cradles my palms, who holds me against them, broken

     /

you're a whole self / and I'm an absence / a suffix of tongue
you're millimeters of bone / and I'm a bear / in the playground
gravel games / you're stealing kisses / and I'm a severed tongue

you're needle / and I'm thighs bruised with sharps / diagnosing myself
queen of metal / you're like lonely / and I'm all like how is having a
body anything but loneliness / you're a sutured veil and I'm
how shame / like grace / instructs us / you're pure
glycerin and I'm / the honey and iron / I mix
with paint / to make it set

      /

my friend and I perch
      at the edge of the reservoir
stare down into blue water
      knived with fish
and tiny teeth of fox
      and fawn
sewn along the slurry bottom
      and I wish
I could hear her heart knocking
      just that close
where the water
      sucks at the absence
of flesh
      confessing my hands
bound to her soft quiet
      I don't call this being alone
          I don't call this being less than whole

ODE TO ASEXUAL LIBIDO

after Margaret F. Browne

the cure for hysteria   finger on clit   throat opening

for wandering womb   hammered into such arterial

gold   afternoon sunlight hot as names in the belly   o gland

            swelling breath   satin stroke   the labial murmur

-ation of birds splintering anxious pupil   into ring

indigo   rain above mountains dilating

                  o hand's wet circle   both disorder of desire

and treatment for   not wanting anyone else   in these sigh hips

        arched into all that penitent   sky pelvis

hinged up and down   the impossible asexual girl ache   faster

        pulse a honeyed lock   gasping   vulva   widening

carnivorous covenant   the uterus flush   and again

that alleviates pain   that reminds how to howl o yes o god killed

and brought back broken   to hum   like a promise   severed

at the daughter o femoral o wrist   o vein pounding with

thirst   if this is first praise   then let every   horizon shudder and spit   the cervix   coughing lightning   back to brain

through the jaws   and thighs sugared   as dirt

o cactus flowers opening   o release   the thunder   into blood

a new   word   for tremble   is burial

ANOTHER X-RAY

Any chance you might be pregnant? When was the last time
you wanted to home against another girl's throat and clavicle,
your mouth taut and mutinous with pearls? What is the name
for a girl who says she doesn't feel attraction, who staves
her belly with powerlines punctured with birds calling
one minor key note over and over? Which arm would you like
me to use to draw blood today? How long have you been
a casket of steroid pills? Do you have a nice boyfriend? Do you
use birth control? May I ask why not? Is ace
one of those new things they've made up these days? What if you
meet the right man and change your mind? Can you
hold still so the technician can try again, please? Can you keep the cross
-hairs of the beam centered on your gut, please?
Are you sure the catheter hurts? Are you sure your gut pain
isn't just because you're on your period right now? You see the red
thread your piss like lead lining honey after the nearby cathedral
burned? Do you know how divided a meteor feels, ligatured blue
with flame up in the breathless cold of a million stars arriving
after their deaths? What's your secret to losing weight?
How often have you found your stool dark lately?
Do you see how your intestine is so obstructed it loops your heart?
When you told your friend you were in hell, did you want
her to come sing you out by holding your tiny wrist, empty
as a halo? Do you know you're in your prime childbearing years?
What if your husband wants kids? Do you know
when they cut you from your mother she briefly regained feeling
and had to try to wake her tongue, like a cicada under snow?
Do you know the sound a dozen hands make in the dark
kneading a mother's belly back into place after the c-section,
of how your tongue is a scar that's proof of the severing?

How many times did your mother teach you to demand
an epidural? How many times did she ask if you imagined kissing girls,
did you imagine lips locking as two people eating matches and silence?
Would you like your mother to draw you churched with morphine
again? What has already begun to nurse your marrow, bladed
with light? When you demanded everyone who love you leave the room
and looked at the NG tube taped to your face, did you call
your dilated pupil a mercury cradle, the hole carved in the shadow
of god that falls across the virgin? Did you call it failure
to tremble for the girl you love, or is that your name
for your ventricles that have learned the art of letting go?
When men running by you yell *nice ass*
do they know the prismatic dark that hungers down the center
of your eyes? The animal jaws you've faithed toward glass
saying *love* like such a desperate woman falling through your bones?

ANOTHER ROADKILL POEM

When we can't drag anything else out of the silence of the plains, I like to play a game called counting birds. Robins are one point, crows two, vultures three. We read the gray landscape for scraps of jet wing, an early jay. Carcasses split open to strands of long red syntax by highway. In the year before I was diagnosed with Crohn's and knew I was aro ace, when all my friends had moved away and I lived alone at the edge of the prairie, I thought I was starving for lack of love. I once climbed into a guy's car just to share breath against my skin. February moon cold as angel cum. Loneliness was a set of hands I sharpened myself against. Once I lied to my doctor that someone was home to make sure I didn't stop breathing after the anesthesia. All the bare trees skied into hungry rust bodies of hawks. When all my friends lived in a canyon, red rocks and knives beneath their pillows to ward off bad luck and strangers, craving thumbs against their throats. I never wanted to be a girl made helpless by anyone's trust, but there was a year I spent chewing my lips and hands like a true carnivore. Ripping up the flesh on my fingers to reveal pink slits of muscle, crusted red craters. There was a year I spent thinking I was a girl worth leaving. Missing you and all our other friends so much tasted like failure. What's the hole, the shape of a life where a partner should go? You sent me photographs of your hair tangled with yellow flowers, books about queerness disrupting time. My family never wanted to articulate what we hold against our wrists and mouths. The great-great-grandmother vanishing into the whole bottle when she couldn't bear to be alone anymore, her husband remarrying the next week. I guess I'm trying to say, in the wings of birds and the mason jar full of silty water and prairie aster on your dashboard, is I trust our commitment to mercy even when we can't language it. When I make paper with my mother again, I pulp my old jeans, black-eyed Susans, your hair. Vulture with its head sunk into the side of each thing smashed on the road's unsentenced tongue.

by the splitting fence post
a broken blue bottle
opens its wings

FOR MY THROAT ON THE MORNING OF A LUNAR ECLIPSE

yes you've seen people on their knees
gagging into the toilet
before sunrise

but it isn't a heartbeat
growing in my belly
when I flush

the colonoscopy prep
I couldn't keep down
magnesium sulfate

salt-sweet false cherry
my friend will ferry me to clinic
I remember last time

fingers laced in lap
of the blue hospital gown
arguing with doctors

telling me steroids
could cinder my fertility
and calcium while saving

my life I said I don't want
children and my father said
you don't know how

quickly your life can change
within weeks my face
swollen luminous

cramp after cramp corkscrewing
my guts in a choked knot
steepled past my heart

bowel blockage often compared
to childbirth
my mother saying

she hates that I go through such pain without even a child at the end

I who never wanted to rest a small pulse on my chest

go outside to watch the winter moon sink red behind the mountains

lavender and black at dawn a fox starved with mange darting

eyes like ambered caskets at me as it runs across the road

without my contacts in the headlights bloom like hot coals

in the dark in a few hours my queer friends will wait for me

while the doctors probe sleep me under to slide a camera into my

intestines this single body of mine partnerless and babyless

and still aromantic is a word doctors can't seem to learn their hands making my empty

guts tear at the slightest touch red stain between my thighs so many ways to be read

AFTER ANOTHER HOSPITAL STAY

I confuse all the trees   for needles
     on these steroids   you fill
a vase with water and prairie aster   late winter rain
     striking the window   like nailheads
I touch   every bruised hole
     across my veins   ringed with adhesive
when I was a girl   my mother taught me
     to draw   the does fleeing the buck
one day the world won't have my body in it
     or yours   one day
I will reach for your palm   and touch cloudshadow
     someone else's thirst   haunting outside
my skeleton   the way I love most
     how these bones run beyond me   full of our soft
and dangerous hearts   the fence
     tangled with the doe   her hooves
another way to pray   with nothing in the mouth
     but how the sky breaks   into branch shadow
on a window   clawed tracks in the dirt
     past the end of the road meadowlark and rusted screws
in the fence post   a light behind the teeth
     across the field across the little twisted spine and blood

QUEERPLATONIC: ALL ASPENS SHARE A HEART SYSTEM

But what are my lungs if not your hands buried in my chest? We sleep
in the mountain's shadow, curled beneath a blanket of horsehair

and stars, kissed with kerosene and dust. Winds trembling daughter
aspens. If your father knew to call this queer, would he break

a wall or into a mouthful of snow? I watch dawn take the peak
from our cabin window, char forged to lake's rippled ache, our blood

still learning to breathe up here, pink grafting granite to black sky, stars.
You rise and run in fog, a cradle of antlers.

If I press your small palm against my side to feel the frantic pulse,
frost will gather on your fingers like a window shocked warm.

If I erode my breath into praise, I can call this a kind of faith.

It is not faith, how a mountain gives up its winter

but the shock of killing warmth, fire hungering the lungs of birds.
If you press a palm to tundra, each blade can take 100 years to pulse

back. My immunosuppressed body catches, lets go of each bright fracture.
Tell me how our blood locks across distances, hips a canyon of hard stars.

Tell me how I can't even say I love you, my girl-mouth a wire in the dark.
I know how to starve for someone's touch. You once scooped a stunned

bird, fingers so thin I saw red light through skin. You folded its trembling
in your hands and snapped its neck. We used to dance in the horse barn.

You gripping my wrists in the old smell of animal sweat.
I've risked sharing my breath with you.

CROWN THIS CHRONIC BODY IN IV TUBES

This poem is a contract between me and you as much as it is a blood machine. A poem like a health insurance agreement, except that if there are gaps or loopholes or exclusions, they are my own. Holes in paragraphs where birds nest like in the spine and pelvis of a fox in a field, violet thread twined around marrow under cloud-blanked sun. These are not meant to trip you up but rather something I have deducted from the text, from the larger blocks. You agree only to what you choose to agree to. I agree to make a document of my mouth, to open my jaw and let you down teeth, tongue, throat, belly. Document in which I say: palm, sky. Document in which I say: it has been seven years since diagnosis, living between sentence and period. Today my chronic body is well. Tomorrow is up for negotiation again.

//

Redwing   after   redwing   returns   after   snow

IV holes leaking a little after the needle is pulled away

my gut fraying to pieces over years little sores pooling little skies

//

gut cramping / that night in a motel / in a small town in the middle of the dark flat plains / scraped by wind / tiny white bathroom with pink grout like / the insides of dead fish / outside stars riveting the dark sky in place / February ice welding rivers shut / frost on the railroad ties passing the meat / plants by the water / where buzzards circle / by day / so I do / what the body asks /and let something howl / through me

//

how I digest insured is responsible for fish riveting meat birth howling

speech act pain deductible red-wind pay premium negotiating the ice
text

//

in the emergency room / between each cramp / when they tell me to
breathe / the doctor asks / if I'm on my period / and when I say yes
/ he says are you sure / these aren't just menstrual pains / eyes on his
clipboard / I say eat shit but under the morphine / it comes out no
um I'm pretty sure no um um / when they remove / my black slacks
/ and underwear / to insert the catheter / so red doesn't stain / my
piss / they leave my black sweater / with the faux pearl buttons / I
wore in school hallways that day / and walk out of the room / to get
blankets / my legs and ass spread / over a red stain / the cath they
said wouldn't hurt / stings like small bees / are honeying my urethra /
with angry punctuation / I think about   / the next doctor
who comes in / cups a hand on my shoulder / when he says / I am not
imagining things / that he is 90% sure / it is full intestinal obstruction
/ due to severe Crohn's Disease / I say / when I repeat this theory /
to every emergency department I visit / in the six weeks / between
first ambulance / and official diagnosis / each doctor sighs / and says /
well I'm not so sure / I'm going to run some more tests to rule / other
possibilities out / each one wheeling me down / the hall / for another
x-ray / a pair of wooden palms on the wall / pressed together / around
a heart / and a cross / a chest that says   /

//

Each person reading the contract shall be under no obligation to swallow

deducting   silence   from   tongue   from   air

morning x-rays liability into tongue and cloud digest sores in gut

//

Policy definitions:

ER   an NG tube threaded through the nose and throat they tell me
       inhale and swallow florescent lights hospital halls alcohol swabs

Colon- syllables lining the vertebrae when the body is put under
oscopy   the tongue thick / numb pupils dilating blank as a tuning fork

Morphine   neck growing weak as a string   on a girl's wrist
         every dream a cupboard full of quiet knife faces

Saline   clear bag dangled above my head like a silent dreamless fish
       slow dripping into my vein with morphine and between pills
       of cipro each little moon chip I cup to my mouth when I ask
       my family to leave me alone for a little while when I tent my
       legs beneath a blue hospital gown and watch headlights stream
       in the road beneath the fifth-level window because sometimes
       I need eyes to not watch me under dress rosetted and puckered
       tied across my back because all salt and water
       flows back to cervix opening

Radiology after I drink contrast mixed with purple grape powder
       they slide me into the machine and tell me it will feel
       like pissing myself but actually it feels like birds
                          up and up and up
         hum heart hum hum hum

//

premium deduct prior digesting authorization wing ray

//

is that your diagnosis are you sure
             you can't eat solid food for weeks drink ensure
we can't approve your medication until we know it's insured
             how would you rate your pain on a 1-10 measure
the tube that makes you cough red is to relieve pressure
             upon review, diagnosis is reassured

//

When the nurse shows me

       how to inject my leg

with the immunosuppressant

       approved by insurance

I don't let her insert the first

       but instead ask her to guide me

with words

       needle punching through skin

and fat teaching my gut

       to stop flaring against itself

and opening me

       to every pollen germ wind

two shots to each thigh

       spaced apart

and then one injection

       every fourteen days, 28-day supply

//

you agree to hold harmless what pre-exists the winter anemic fault lines

//

it's been seven years / of needles / since the last ambulance / since we took a car instead / to save on costs / racing ahead of morphine / to a larger hospital / ahead of a paragraph naming / me on a list of exclusions / to a HIPAA authorization / and agreement to pay insurance fees / each paper / a horse lunging / across water / since I stood in the shower / using orange shampoo all-in-one / to clean the grease / and IV adhesive / scooped against my neck / and followed a team of doctors back to my room / who talked about me / in the third person / as an interesting and rare case study / fascinating to see / the damage / until I said gentlemen / it's nice to meet you / and stuck out my hand / their faces pivoting around / staring horses / and every year since / my risk of cancer / goes up statistically / like grass / in a field

//

Anxiety triggers someone posts they have cancer after years on my meds
                    someone tells me pregnancy would cure my symptoms
                    someone tells me I could have prevented my illness
                    someone tells me oranges and blueberries can cure things
                    someone tells me sex would reduce my anxiety
                    someone tells me yucca and agave bloom from guts

//

co-pay shatters the tube fees hipaa proof of income for tax purposes proof
   of   flowers prior authorization is required please contact

your   hoofs allow up to 48 hours   a changes to
     do you feel your medication is improving your

symptoms or helping them stay   the   claim   processed   for
     pollen germ until bill is generated you will be responsible for

river do you smoke do you drink any chance you might be pregnant
     do you have   coverage someone to drive you home

//

There's a problem with my insurance authorization
                              so I'm circling the kitchen in hot mountain
sunlight, stuck on hold [*ma'am please*]
              lightning crackling and blotting the call center person
                    every few words
                                          three yellow flowers
              in a vase of water on the kitchen table
late winter ice-eater winds over mountains   [*you need to call*]
        foothills scrubby with purple sage
                        blue peaks capped in snow
        I circle and circle the small kitchen thinking [*another
department*]
of the wild horses that gallop   in the fields past the highway
                              a couple hours from here
their pale bodies in the night
                        a circle of breaths
                              [*there's a problem processing your
insurance*]
                    past broken fences and corrals splintered with nails
[*please call another department*]
                              black silhouettes of mountains
        where manes and tails turn in a wheel
              [*ma'am I understand you're upset*]
                                    the sound of hooves
vanishing into grass   [*ma'am I have a daughter with Crohn's
too*]
        where I wake up with a horse's scapulae across my face
                    [*her Crohn's got better when she got pregnant*]
clouds inside of jaw
        [*ma'am are you still there ma'am*]
                        purple flowers threaded through holes
        and my mouth
              a red cliff the horses leap from

//

    each vein   blows open under needle pressure like a contract
guts touch the birds   pressure moon   enough light cannot be
    responsible for from beneath   sage blue   what pre-exists
      the hoofs   holes forgotten my insurance
   I say   jaw scrub   wind hold lightning
I am partly dependent on   like me river   do what you leave
       but tube threaded through   manes little pill little cliff doesn't
stain   flying your tongue
     ghosted globeflower   the vertebrae   spine blooms
document   of intestinal please   my hips to scream
     in the shadow remember   pain you can't eat red

//

cover me cover I cover   me I   cover me   me I cover me I
me I cover you   cover me you I cover me you I I I cover
I cover you cover you cover you coveryoucoveryoucoveryou

//

In remission

                I cross a snowmelt-swollen glacial creek

on horseback

                its mane snapping

when it tosses its head and blows

                at the top of the hill

swivels its head toward mule deer

                that flare their nostrils

at our wild scent

                snort and run into the aspen trees

above the fire line

                studded with needles

rain line moving toward us

                if lightning approaches

I am to climb off the horse

                and let the bolt strike its hot flanks

BECAUSE I LIVE IN A GIRL'S SKELETON THIS ONCE

the gynecologist presses her palm against my belly, searching for a sign
of tumor forty-two days in bleeding. This morning a clot filled my hand
the size of a baby mouse, smell like cold metal
or stream. When vaginismus drags a scream from me
she puts ice water rags across my throat and tells me to breathe
fill each lung slow, let the pelvis relax, the hips fall
so far open I could be a sky, a red cloud full of the sound
of rain and teeth. So much blood she can't
see to the back of my uterus, her hands
searching inside the childless and breathless blessing
of arch, swallowed song. O friend, o darling,
o sister-sweet with violets woven in your jaws, be with me
here: red after red spilling between my thighs like the wing
I found rocking before my door one day, tether
twisted around knob wrenched from socket. The empty body
gone in the early spring rain, wind tugging the blue-gray feathers
where I met my reflection in glass. Blood rapture of one ovary
then another pressed in her hand, cradle-bruised quicksilver burial
ground. And here, again, instead of a god of cord and covenant, I turn
to you like you could sew your hands across every hole in this
dangerous sky. Not baby but elegy pearled from nitrate and albumen
in the gentle of your fingers. If I lick this red from my hands
will I be born again with the right hungers this time,
flooding until she spills a trackless night back between star
and ache? If the rib cage in the prairie dotted by yellow flowers
like a crib not far from here, if a highway where every faith
is red across the asphalt, what then do I call down through me
into the circle we make of our hands, a pelvic bone
ringing the flood, the iron, the wreck we choose in each other
again and again?

ELEGY FOR MY MOTHER

I'm sorry, mother, to write you as if you were dead
again. It's only that I tried to imagine it—
your body on a table for me to prepare
your ashes in a jar for me to carry on my dashboard—
and couldn't.
Instead, our hands stretched over the electric fence,
the nervous mares pushing their muzzles
into our palms.
Instead, your mother's gold watch
stopped against your wrist, your hand
guiding ice chips to her mouth.
I'm sorry I've been such a hungry throat.
I'm sorry for the C-section scar.
Sorry to always be thinking of the coyote song
you listen to when you walk back alone
to your car at night, of when you wrapped the milk-mouthed kit
in a grease-stained towel. I'm trying to say
I want your arms always, I'm trying to say
that I imagine arranging your hair, your breasts,
your stretch-marked skin, and I thought
of the vulture I saw on the clifftop
swooping between me
and a blue horizon.
Maybe it's how you cupped my hands
around the dragonfly
after we drowned it
to try to keep the color—how you painted
each faded blue spot back on, showing me
that sometimes the only way
we know how to keep something
is to kill it
so we don't have to bear watching it
vanish one breath at a time without us
in daylight.

AFTER THE RN WARNS ME ABOUT THE BLOOD

—so much the pap smear might not be able to catch cancer—after I push
myself onto my elbows alone in the room and try to clean
off the red smudged across my belly, after the masked phlebotomist
cinches a strip of black medical tape around my arm and tells me
her plans to go home and cook dinner with her brother
when her shift is done in five minutes, after I keep thinking
about the nurse who offered to sterilize me because I knew best
if I wanted another soft fontanelle breaking
into the world through me, after I fold my diagnosis
of *menhorragia, > three months* and walk almost all the way home
by the highway during the 4:30pm Friday rush hour, after a man
with a rattlesnake tattoo gives me a ride the rest of the way,
after I don't tell my mother, after I walk to work the following Monday
on a sidewalk so slick with wet pink petals I nearly slip
on their sweet skin, after I crouch in my office
with the door closed and open my knees
to try to push the clots through, after I watch a young man
in glasses wrestle and sweat to plant young plum trees
in the parking lot median, after I think about
my compromised immune system holding me open
to each thing that could kill me—each way someone doesn't care enough
about this to change some small thing in their day,
in the way their palms or their breath touch—after I start crying
into my keyboard, after my boss offers to drive me home
and admits he was not well sheltering in place this winter
either, after he says it is okay not to be okay,
after he tells me to sleep in a dark room and take the next day off
too if needed, after I put my arm across my eyes
and remember dancing with girls in the armory, how I saw
my pale face nerveless and remote as a moon in the bathroom lights,

after I remember the girl who kissed each of her palms
and pressed them to my cheeks, after I remember
the six-foot-five boy who cupped his gentle hands
like two halves of a pomegranate when he sat
on the edge of my roommate's bed, after I remember
hearing he was gone, when I had to pull over
onto the dirt shoulder of the road
beneath the billboard with Jesus on one side
and a pregnant belly on the other
above the field of harvested dusk,
and I remember all the times I begged god
to keep all my friends alive just another hour just another day,
like the words could hold onto the bunched backs of their shirts
and keep them here just like this—stay,
stay with me, please, just another minute—
after I name each thing I can't save
but before the results come back
I text you: *please tell me*
you're on your way.

ENDINGS TO POEMS ABOUT GRIEF I CANNOT BEGIN

because in the months without touch
there was nothing but missing you, friend, nothing
but ache to hold you, but menstruating thick as candle wax,
but how you said my name
like the opposite of infection and T cell blooming,
us talking each other through each month with our faces pixeled
into wound, how I couldn't bear to let myself love you
—skin-hungry and unjawed as a snake—
and you loved me anyway.

*

how she licked her fawn's ear in dawn ash, how leaf-shaped soot
from the forest fire struck me right here in the sternum, where your arm
grafts my chest to you.

*

both of us counting all our losses in our uncut hair.

*

when the midwives open us, do they hold the grief in our hips
as gently as we do for each other?

*

I am that animal
dragging herself to the warm weight of friends
like you, how my chest is a pneumatic hive of breath and blood honey
rhyming matchstick with marrow and forest burned
with the small of my back, a place for you to cry.

*

we have loved each other so many years
and still we are learning the language to say *I*
invite you in, I trust with my sinew, womb, collar
—o star harness. you can always come home to this

perishing light though it is.

*

the disaster we took as *future*, as *some time*
has been unfurling its radiant ruin all along
beside us, all along our *now* kindling hoofs in my lungs,
thirst in the prickly pear spines we mistook for nipples.

*

quiet as a bone
you take my hand.

*

because if lightning gathers above us on horseback
we are supposed to climb off the mares' warm bodies
and let the bolts strike them instead. because sometimes
we have no choice but to ground ourselves, to love ourselves enough
to love someone else. because we can rest our breath in each other
and trust the light that comes in all its fierce untethering.

*

—but instead, for you, just because you're blueing a little today
I'd cut my mouth on wind
blowing the bluestem flat in snow,
sever my tongue and press it against your jaw
to fever down the words, press a steaming mug
into your palms. snow into a womb, hold bruise
-eyed chicks in my mouth for you. make a nest for our bodies
of steel and paper, tight as a knife
in a jealous boy's pocket.

*

after I bled into a woman's hands,
I sent you a card of a pressed yucca blossom
because I knew you were hurting, because I wanted you to know
you were loved. if you cup my shoulder, I will warm your palm
like a blue glass candle. I will keep finding ways to love you,

to beg more time of this sky stained with the lungs of birds
bending hunger to absent meridian, all these cicadas' desperate faith
singing such unmiraculous extinction.

*

ash falling into your lungs, another medical bill in your hands.
I just
want to cover you.

*

the drawing of a trachea I made in health class, the body a loop
of graphite on butcher paper, the salmon-spill of belly
sketched rough but steady, the way my mother taught me:
one continuous line, an attention that, nonetheless, will not save us.

*

and I
keep measuring the time that is left by the length
of your ribs, by each year I have learned to open myself
more to you. the shelter we make of each other.

THE OPPOSITE OF TOUCH-STARVED IS BEING A THEREMIN OF THROAT AND WIND

because you were never taught to say yes / to her offered palm

because loving a girl openly / has always felt like an apology

because once you saw yourself in a photograph / standing next to
    someone / her face nuzzling your ear / and you tore it in half

because you once huddled in a room / with a hundred other girls
    watching a speaker draw a diagram / against *homosexual impulses*

because it shames you to want / to hide your face / between her shoulder
    and neck / weeping until she calls you / good again

because when she says she loves you / believe her

because you dream of sewing all her love letters / to your ribs / like a
corset / sleepless as a platelet / that holds the wound / shut

because once you prayed / by begging god to rip her name from your
     mouth like bitterroot

because she pressed her face / between your shoulder blades / to hug
     your heart / through your spine

because you want to be taken to the place / where even the animals come
     to die / to offer their throats for the knife / in the safest place of
     all next to / her ribs

because she helps you find your breath / in all 98.2 degrees of her blood
     against the snow-flecked wind / carving these plains
     and come home to her

because you woke in the body / of the queer person you were always
     afraid of

because she says you hold her

because you learned to pray / by saying your name / the way she says it
    like something that belongs only to her

because once you couldn't bear / to be someone who needed
    to be touched

because loving her is not an x-ray / not every needle shadow in your
    arms / but walking knee-deep through bluestem / hand on hip

because being loved by her / is neck morphine-weak in hospital bed
    is the wet stone she stole / from the river for you

because you are torn haunch / and broken headlight
    every morning now

because she buys you books of poems / she can't afford / just because
   they remind her of you

because she gives your words back to you / like drunk bees / sugar-
   radared home / laying her four-chambered animal next to yours

because you want / to know how to say yes to loving yourself so much
   you can let yourself love another woman / out loud

because you want / to tell this woman / this poem
is heat shimmer / above the blacktop
        is the canyon wall / where you hid all your cries
                for her / is sun skinning prickly pear
is an amen you keep splitting
                / down the sternum   to thrumming   /
                        you want   /
        to tell her that she can / always come home to you
                that she taught you to admit you need kindness enough
                        to collapse open   /
                into such a bare church of bone / for her to hide inside

because be still tender ruin

because to learn how to hold someone else / you begin with yourself

because you press your thumbs / to your carotid
    until you feel your tongue

because you stand by the river / and press your forehead / to hers

because she calls you her Joshua tree / and stars fall out of your mouth

because morning makes a salt memory of you / because when she says
    her own name / you feel it in a nerve at the nape of your neck

because letting yourself be loved / is a five a.m. dressed in plaid and
    bone / gasoline and plains wind / sky the color of a gutted fish

because there is no god on the highway / except how she
    squeezes your hand / and turns the radio up louder

because like a cocoon / rewrites her hungers / you are fluid
    as a language

because you love the lullaby of barbwire / and soft bone of this woman

because you follow her breath down / to the night that holds you

because you run your palms down your vertebrae / until you love her
    too

because you let this body you are / finally north to someone's blue because you want to be as good / as she tells you / you are

because with her / the wings that fill your pelvis / will always bleed

DEER SKULL FLOATING OVER BLUE MOUNTAINS (FOUR PANELS)

i.

Something like want but not   for the body
how I look at a person and feel nothing most of the time
       except a desire to touch the wrist   of someone tired
who has said kind things to me
to want to blurt *I love that you trust me*
       that you look at me with such a full attention   asking   nothing
of me
and instead say *I'm sorry someone treated you like shit*
We're home in how we listen
I don't want to fuck or be fucked by anyone
I just want to hide safe in your heart cavity
I just want you to be well to love each sharp tooth in your throat as
yours
How we all want to be made landscape with vertebrae
       someone could study with interest for hours
What I know from paintings of the virgin in her robe
       —*prude church girl stuck-up bitch* god how I have to keep saying
aroace
       is how some blues fade over time to just the lead
If I start licking the cobalt from your vein now in a hundred years it will
fade inside me to a ghost I can't stop loving

ii.

I'm sorry I could never soften a space inside me for the folks

who wanted me   the ones who leaned back against the railing

     of the fossil ashbed where we worked

     or asked if I wanted to dance after months of being friends

each time I said no to the question of laying beside each other

     I wanted to cup that face turning away from me

   jaw tightening wanted to say *thank you for making me feel worth the*

risk

I am whittling us out of whatever light's left

of an unearthed horse mounted on this wall above the ashbed

and thinking of the dreams I've had the last few nights under desert stars of platonic touch: a palm pressed my back

      during birth   someone embracing me when I am naked

      in the shower her black shirt sleeve scraping my ear

      someone offering their warm arm to help me down the stairs

I love when someone is turned away from me

      so fully absorbed in what they're thinking how they're breathing

When I see a deer I smell my mother

      painting a skull on a deep blue background

      wind in the sockets dark hollows of fosse of cranium

iii.

Did you know that I drew you, friend?   Your throat steepling

      blue sky with the long drop of a raven

welled like ink   our minds are something akin to one another

      Friend we are used to making space only for others

I cut open your heart: there's nothing

to be afraid of   rattlesnake

babies nesting warm in your   chambers each of your pulses a wall

coaxing them to sleep   onyx into   juniper through

      highway unto   tendon undone by sun

      we don't have to kiss   anybody

      Sorry what was I saying

it's just that you slid into the room on soft socks

just that you started humming that song again   without even realizing it's just your t-shirt with the holes in it

No one I love is mine   and this is what I love most

about living   even though

knowing each name   means missing someone

no one and nothing we love belongs to us   not even our breath

I can love you because I live alone and can go hide my spine in glacier

We can rest against my sick guts

     my belly a red rock wall ending in stars nail points in a night sky

     where dragonflies dart where I could catch each one hide it

       between your shoulderblades for safekeeping

iv.

My mother has spent a lifetime trying to draw her mother

as a skull and I have spent a lifetime trying to draw her

   gray threads of hair from out of my mouth

   her spotted hands tapping a paint brush four times on

   my back bristles dabbing cadmium cerulean lavender foothills

I have tried to distill everything down to this

the sun sparing nothing on the canvas

   my mother drawing me morphined in the hospital bed

   closing the studio door again after I asked love's question

   so I had to watch her paint through the gaps in the hinges

I am painting a vagina I am painting my mother

I am making a page

      I hold my body and its word

      giving it space breath like she taught me

don't pull back the white sheet from the canvas she's working on

learn to read the shadows the undercoat of blue

   the lines she has drawn erased drawn again

   gray heel prints from her lead-coarsened hand

ON BEING THE QUEER PERSON
I WAS ALWAYS AFRAID I'D BE

when you breathe on the bed next to me
I remember when I went searching for wild foxes

because I didn't want to keep holding your name under my tongue
until it killed me. Because I tried so hard not to love you, let you love me

but like the skinned heifer that fell off the back of the truck
that the flies found in the middle of the road near my house

I was zipped into such a sequined blood-humming
for you. You, hematite mercy in me

a lodestone I can find any time
I lose my way. This poem a home I've tried to make for you

the way I hold everything soft in my belly,
every highway where barbed wire stitches the winter clouds shut

looping across my hips, knees, sacrum. If you open your eyes
if you take my wrist's pulse between your fingers,

the canyon's frozen river will bloom purple lupine
right out of the ice, each valve in my chest a place you can hide

your unholiest prayers. You give me back to myself, make me
what I am, the way breath and flesh join at the sternum. Why

is it so hard just to say it, just to choir our tongues into words
all the fathers in our lives never wanted us

to learn? Before I met you, a woman accused me of my mouth
before I knew what it meant, before I knew if I wanted

to be her or be close to her, or that I was ace. And the rarest of times
I've thought I felt something for a girl, I learned to hold my breath

for you. Because it would've been easier just to stop my mouth
the way I stopped my hands from tightening your black peacoat

around you when it snowed around us in that prairie city,
we shared the list of hurt we carry, and I didn't pull you

into a hug so tight it crushed your coffee cup between us—
but now you say it and press your palms to my sick belly, the x-rays

of my gut looping up past my heart, the needle bruises in my thighs
where I have to wound myself every other week to stay alive.

I couldn't find any foxes because they all died of mange.
So call this what it is—how you move toward me

first, how you say it when I can't. Lace your fingers with mine
across my navel—call this a cauterized moon,

the place where I separated from my mother's body
to find yours. Call this belief blush and maxilla, index of fevers,

call it fossil that remembers water enough to be soft. Call it vein
encrypted with your voice, rhapsody of ghost, call it how I'll always

come find you, call it so loud we can't hear all the people
grafting scripture to the air against the local Pride club

hosting a drag show to beat cancer. Call it
my immune system turning your hands gliding over me

to cloud shadow. Call it how language lives in a warm place inside you
and you invite me there. Because to be loved

by someone's throat is to let the wind take you to your knees, to worry you're enough to depend upon. The heart an animal staggering away

from the road to the field of snow. Call

her name and see how fast this beast can run
to your side. If you—if we—want to.

If we let each other in. If we stay. If we say it
there's no going back. If your cheekbones are telephone wires splitting

dawn into stanzas of birds. If you open their singing inside me.
If you hold me here, one hand on my clavicle, against the cold,

if we can hug each other through the ribs like it's enough.

INSTEAD OF CHEWING A HOLE IN MY LIP &
SWALLOWING THE BLOOD

let's say rain before dawn   say the dead fox in the meadow   say you

come to tell me of it   say cloud and chest   hollow around

heart   say purple gayfeather   say I ask you to tell me the skull

and I draw your face   say you touch the softest part   of my throat

say you slide a knife into my belly   and gut me

gently lift out each organ   and weigh it in your hands   set each one

aside   until I fall to pearl   and pink glisten

slicking your fingers   say you cup my eyes   and call each one

beautiful   say you cradle my lungs   say you breathe for both of us

my skeleton waking up hitched   to your morning field

grass beneath the thunder   say you call me   your little moon

your little lupine root   your animal gentled   to your voice

with a hand on my neck   say your words   give me back to myself

say our mothers call   asking if we're okay   say needles

line the fridge   like latches   to my blood

say a little red pools   inside a mouth   say today I am still alive

say today I do not chew my way   through the tender traps

of palm and mercy say the sky   full of tongue   after tongue

still singing   every way there is to hold   a pulse

NOTES

"Ode to Asexual Libido" was influenced by the general body of work and poetic ethos of the poet Margaret F. Browne. It was not inspired by any one particular poem of Browne's.

"Explication of the Poet's Breasts" was partly influenced both by Paisley Rekdal's "Nightingale: A Gloss" and Jenny Boully's *The Body: An Essay*. "Crown this Chronic Body in IV Tubes" was partly influenced by the work of Solmaz Sharif.

The italicized phrase near the opening of "Letter to an Incel from an Ace Girl" comes from a widely-circulated quote from an incel who posted online about following a teenage girl until "she ran like a newborn fawn." The poem also generally engages with incel language.

& ACKNOWLEDGMENTS

And one more meadow—thank you all, loves, for supporting this book and making it possible, starting with you, the person reading this book.

Thank you Mary Jo Bang for your beautiful reading of these poems, for choosing this book. Thank you so much to Rusty Morrison, Ken Keegan, and Laura Joakimson, some of the kindest, loveliest people I have ever met—I can't thank you enough for your time and your attention to these poems. Thank you for believing in this book. Thank you also to everyone on the Omnidawn team who helped bring this book into being in the form you now find it and for dedicating so much hard work to it. One of the sweetest pleasures of writing a book is, I think, the way it both grows in relationship with others—the way a manuscript becomes woven into friendship and correspondence and reflects our loves— and the way it also facilitates relationships, becomes another way of engaging and finding chosen family. Thank you all at Omnidawn for being part of my—and this book's—ecological community.

Thank you so much to Mary Jo Bang, Dan Beachy-Quick, Rosebud Ben-Oni, and Emma Bolden for the generosity of your words about this book.

My boundless gratitude to the first people who so generously read and provided feedback to this book: Rosebud Ben-Oni, John James, and Rebecca Starks. Thank you so much for your kind words, your sharp insight, your excellent revision suggestions, your professional advice in publishing and promoting and beyond, and your ongoing support. You are all so kind and such keen readers, and I am so glad this book has reached its final form because of your astute suggestions.

Thank you, always, to my dear friends at the Colorado State University MFA program, both fellow students and teachers, who taught me so much and have laid the foundation for everything in my writing and publishing life since. Thank you Susannah Lodge-Rigal and Kristin Macintyre for the ongoing poetry correspondence and our community together. Special thanks to Dan Beachy-Quick, Sasha Steensen, Harrison Candelaria Fletcher, and Stephanie G'Schwind, always, for their close mentorship throughout my time at CSU. And thank you, always, to my dear friends at Wayne State College and Northeast Community College, who invited me into the writing world in the first place, the first poetry community I found—you welcomed me and gave me space to exist as myself, before I even found the language for my queerness. Thank you, also, to the many writers the WSC and NECC folks introduced me to—all of you brought me into community and home. Special thanks to JV Brummels and Tim and Cindy Black. Thank you to Allison Hedge Coke for signing one of the first books of poetry I ever owned and writing "give it a push and get the work out there."

Particular gratitude to Margaret F. Browne and Michelle Thomas, fellow Colorado State MFA folks, and to Stephanie Hempel and Derek Pufahl, fellow Wayne State College folks: everything I write is always in conversation with all of you. Sitting on living room floors, talking with you, considering the kind of lives we want to live as artists, the way we want to exist in the world—our friendship has shaped me for a lifetime. Everything I write is a letter to all of you in some way. You are such stunning writers and thinkers and friends. I love you all so much. (And Michelle and Stephanie, I am forever in your debt for your wise and kind social media and marketing advice and generous help. Thank you thank you thank you.)

For the ongoing queer conversation and kinship, thank you Carol Guess and Lucien Darjeun Meadows and C. E. Janecek, living such thoughtful lives in addition to offering such kind words and helping these poems live in the world. Thank you to my fellow editors Daniel Schonning and Geoffrey Babbitt for teaching me so much as we work together as a team. And thank you Allison Adair, Kasey Jueds, Claire Boyles, and the many more writers along the way with whom I've read, learned, interviewed, and more.

To Justin Hargett: thank you thank you thank you thank you for all of your hard work and knowledge in supporting this book in the world.

Thank you so much, Abby, for your incredible friendship and love. Thank you Elly, Jennie, Erin, Alie, Brandon, Liz, Sara, Bill, Gordon, Mykah, Sahian, Kate, Shannon for being such a kind and supportive community—to quote Liz, "you make my heart shine." Thank you Deborah for helping me stay grounded and find calm.

Thank you, always, to my parents, for all of your love and friendship. Thank you for being artists with me. Thank you for your support when I came out as a poet. Thank you for your support when I came out again as queer (each time & ever & always).

Thank you to all the people I cannot name here, including anyone I may have forgotten by mistake and the many, many writers—here and gone—who have influenced me over the years.

Thank you to the editors of the publications in which some of these poems first appeared, sometimes in slightly different form. Special thank you to Kristina Marie Darling, for all of your incredible editorial support and work in addition to featuring my work at the *Best American Poetry* blog, and to Emma Bolden, for your insightful interview questions for that blog and also all of your support along the way. Thank you for being some of the best readers I could ever ask for. Thank you also to the editors of some of these publications who offered excellent feedback to help make these poems what they are today.

AGNI: "Portait of the Chest as Fogged Miror and Ballpoint Tattoo"
Best American Poetry Poet Spotlight: "Instead of Another X-Ray," "Portrait of Crib with Coyote Skull Inside," "Endings to Poems About Grief I Cannot Begin," "Queerplatonic: All Aspens Share a Heart System," "On Being the Queer Person I Was Always Afraid I'd Be"
Electric Literature's *The Commuter:* "Another X-Ray," "Elegy for My

Mother"

Frontier 2021 Open Finalist: "Jokes Only Asexuals Will Understand {Click Link to Open New Page}"

Fourteen Poems: "Ode to the Drift Glass Necklace My Friend Gave Me"

Foglifter: "Portrait as Mid-2000s Girl Without a Boyfriend"

Gulf Coast Online: "Explication of the Poet's Breasts"

Hayden's Ferry Review: "Nocturne with Keys Clenched Between Knuckles" was featured in the Body Language online series

Interim: "How to Draw Yourself as Daughter"

Nimrod: "Ode to His Knife Collection"

Pleiades: "For My Throat on the Morning of a Lunar Eclipse," selected as a finalist for the 2022 Prufer Prize

Salamander: "Blood Firsts," "Snake-Jawed Epithalamium" (with gratitude to the editors for the Pushcart Prize nomination for "Blood Firsts")

Waxwing: "Another Roadkill Poem," "After Another Hospital Stay," "Because I Live in a Girl's Skeleton This Once," "After the RN Warns Me About the Blood," and "When I Watched My Mother Paint."

And, as it began, thank you. Always, always you, here in the field of grass and bone where we meet to join hands once again.

Kelly Weber (she/they) is the author of *We Are Changed to Deer at the Broken Place* (Tupelo Press, 2022). She is the reviews editor for *Seneca Review* and has been nominated for the Pushcart Prize. Their work has appeared or is forthcoming in a *Best American Poetry* Author Spotlight, *Gulf Coast Online*, Electric Literature's *The Commuter*, *Hayden's Ferry Review Online*, *Southeast Review*, *Salamander*, *The Journal*, and elsewhere. She holds an MFA from Colorado State University.

You Bury the Birds in My Pelvis

by Kelly Weber

Cover art by Emily Goodheart

Cover design byLaura Joakimson

Interior design by Laura Joakimson and Kelly Weber

Cover typeface: Marian

Interior typeface: Marian and Hightower

Printed in the United States
by Books International, Dulles, Virginia

Publication of this book was made possible in part by gifts from Katherine
& John Gravendyk in honor of Hillary Gravendyk, Francesca Bell, Mary
Mackey, and The New Place Fund

Omnidawn Publishing Oakland, California

Staff and Volunteers, Fall 2023

Rusty Morrison, senior editor & co-publisher
Laura Joakimson, executive director and co-publisher
Rob Hendricks, poetry & fiction editor, & post-pub marketing
Jason Bayani, poetry editor
Anthony Cody, poetry editor
Liza Flum, poetry editor
Kimberly Reyes, poetry editor
Sharon Zetter, poetry editor & bookdesigner
Jeffrey Kingman, copy editor
Jennifer Metsker, marketing assistant
Sophia Carr, marketing assistant
Katie Tomzynski, marketing assistant